Handy Delaware Genealogy Handbook

By Gary L. Morris

ISBN-13: 978-1506191591

ISBN-10: 1506191592

Table of Contents

Notes

Genealogical Research in Delaware

Delaware is known as the "Diamond State," and some genealogical gems can certainly be found there. There are many historical and genealogical records available for Delaware but you won't have to dig too much for them; we'll show you exactly where they are. To get you started in tracing your Delaware ancestry, we'll introduce you to those records, and help you to understand:

1. What they are
2. Where to find them
3. How to use them

These records can be found both online and off, so we'll introduce you to online websites, indexes and databases, as well as brick-and-mortar repositories and other institutions that will help with your research in Delaware. So that you will have a more comprehensive understanding of these records, we have provided a brief history of the "Diamond State" to illustrate what type of records may have been generated during specific time periods. That information will assist you in pinpointing times and locations on which to focus the search for your Delaware ancestors and their records.

A Brief History of Delaware

The first Europeans to settle in Delaware were a group of Swedes under the leadership of Peter Minuits. Minuits was the first governor of New York, and the Swedish group broke away from the Dutch to establish their own colony. The Dutch had other ideas however, as they laid claim to the area. The two nations fought for control, each by establishing forts in various strategic locations. The Dutch built Fort Nassau near Camden and the on the site of present-day Newcastle, the Swedes established bases at Tinicum and Lewiston. The Dutch finally prevailed in 1655, overthrowing the Swedish fortifications and claiming the entire area for Holland.

The Dutch ruled the region until 1664 when the English overthrew them and Delaware was united with New York. In 1682 the area between Newcastle and Cape Henlopen was sold to William Penn by the Duke of York, and this area constitutes the modern-day state of Delaware. Delaware was governed as part of Pennsylvania until the time of the American Revolution, though they had enough liberty from the governor of Pennsylvania to form their own distinct assembly.

Delaware was among the thirteen colonies which initiated the American Revolution against the British, and adopted its own constitution in 1776 at which time it declared itself the "Delaware State." Delaware officially became a state on December 7, 1787. At the time of the Civil War, Delaware was rare in that it was a Union state that still practiced slavery. Though divided, the state elected not to secede from the Union, and though its troops mainly fought for the union cause, some served in Delaware companies on the Confederate side.

Delaware never formally abolished slavery, though after the war the majority of slave owners freed their slaves voluntarily. The state voted against the 13th Amendment to abolish slavery, however accepted its institution and slavery was abolished in the state in 1865. Delaware finally ratified the Amendment in 1901, forty years after the Emancipation Proclamation.

Important Genealogical Dates in Delaware History

- **1638** – Colony of New Sweden founded

- **1654** – Dutch colonists conquer New Sweden

- **1664** – British conquer the Dutch and take control of
- Delaware

- **1682** – First Quaker settlements

- **1703** – Establishes separate provincial assembly, though remains under the jurisdiction of the Governor of Pennsylvania

- **1787** – Becomes a state of the United States

- **1740** – majority of the state organized into towns

- **1777** – British forces raid Danbury

- **1788** – Statehood

- **1792** – Adopts second state constitution and changes its name to the State of Delaware

- **1865** – State votes against 13th Amendment

- **1920** – Delaware women receive complete suffrage

Famous Battles Fought in Delaware

There was only one land battle fought in Delaware during the Revolutionary War, and a minor naval skirmish in Delaware Bay. Although only a few, these battle accounts can be very effective in uncovering the military records of your ancestor. They can tell you what regiments fought in which battles, and often include the names and ranks of many officers and enlisted men. Following are the two most famous battles fought in Delaware and links to useful information about them.

Battle of Cooch's Bridge, 1777

Battle of Cooch's:
http://www.ushistory.org/march/phila/tobrandywine_4.htm

Battle of Delaware Bay, 1782

Battle of Delaware Bay: http://www.revolutionary-war-and-beyond.com/joshua-barney-wins-battle-of-delaware-bay.html

Common Delaware Genealogical Issues and Resources to Overcome Them

Boundary Changes: Boundary changes are a common obstacle when researching Delaware ancestors. You could be searching for an ancestor's record in one county when in fact it is stored in a different one due to historical county boundary changes. The **Atlas of Historical County Boundaries** can help you to overcome that problem. It provides a chronological listing of every boundary change that has occurred in the history of Delaware.

Atlas of Historical County Boundaries:
http://publications.newberry.org/ahcbp/documents/DE_Consolidated _Chronology.htm#Consolidated_Chronology

Name Changes: Surname changes, variations, and misspellings can complicate genealogical research. It is important to check all spelling variations. Soundex, a program that indexes names by sound, is a useful first step, but you can't rely on it completely as some name variations result in different Soundex codes. The surnames could be different, but the first name may be different too. You can also find records filed under initials, middle names, and nicknames as well, so you will need to **get creative with surname variations** and spellings in order to cover all the possibilities. For help with surname variations read our instructional article on **How to Use Soundex**.

get creative with surname variations :
http://obituarieshelp.org/blog/?p=634

How to Use Soundex : http://obituarieshelp.org/blog/?p=505

Delaware Genealogical Organizations and Archives

Genealogical resources include not only records, but the organizations that house them, or can direct you to them. These institutions include: *Archives, Libraries, Genealogical Societies, Family History Centers, Universities, Churches, and Museums.*

Following are links to their websites, their physical addresses, and a summary of the records you can find there.

Archives

Delaware Public Archives – vital records, apprentice indentures, church records, historical newspapers, bastardy bonds, death register, naturalization records, probate records, orphan records

Delaware Public Archives
121 Martin Luther King Jr. Blvd. North
Dover, DE 19901
Tel: 302-744-500
Fax: 302-739-2578
Email: aarchives@state.de.us

Delaware Public Archives: http://archives.delaware.gov/

Dover Public Library – historical documents, maps, newspapers

City Hall
15 Loockerman Plaza,
Dover, DE 19901
Tel: (302)-736-7030

Dover Public Library: http://www.cityofdover.com/Home-Library/

University of Delaware Library – rare books, manuscripts, state and local histories, family and personal papers of Delawareans, archival records of Delaware organizations

University of Delaware Library
181 South College Avenue
Newark, DE 19717-5267
Tel: 302-831-2965

University of Delaware Library: http://www.lib.udel.edu/ud/spec/

South Coastal Public Library – various genealogical resources
43 Kent Avenue
Bethany Beach, DE 19930
Tel: (302) 539-5231

South Coastal Public Library: http://www.southcoastal.lib.de.us/

Delaware Genealogical and Historical Societies

Genealogical and historical societies have access to extensive catalogues of genealogical data. They are also able to offer expert guidance for genealogical researchers. Many members are professional genealogists who are most willing to share their expertise in finding ancestors.

The Historical Society of Delaware Library - Delaware genealogies, manuscripts, reference files, newspapers, maps, and historical and cultural photographs

505 North Market Street,
Wilmington DE 19801-3091
Tel: (302)-655-7161

The Historical Society of Delaware Library: http://www.hsd.org/

Delaware Genealogical Society – various resources and instructional material

Delaware Genealogical Society
505 North Market Street
Wilmington DE 19810-3091

Delaware Genealogical Society link to: http://delgensoc.org/

Downstate Delaware Genealogical Society – various genealogical resources

P.O. Box 1787
Dover, DE 19903-1787
Email: info@downstatedegenealogists.org

Downstate Delaware Genealogical Society:
http://www.downstatedegenealogists.org/

Sussex County Genealogical Society – various genealogical resources, surnames research list

c/o Rehoboth Beach Public Library
226 Rehoboth Avenue
Rehoboth Beach, DE 19971

Sussex County Genealogical Society:
http://www.scgsdelaware.org/

Marvel Museum – historical photographs, newspaper clippings, books and other Delaware memorabilia

510 S. Bedford St.
Georgetown, DE 19947

Marvel Museum: http://www.marvelmuseum.com/

New Castle Historical Society – historical photographs, books, manuscripts, works-on-paper, and documents spanning over three hundred years of local Delaware and national history.

New Castle Historical Society:
http://www.newcastlehistory.org/houses/collections.html

Delaware Family History Centers

The Family History Centers run by the LDS Church offer free access to billions of genealogical records for free to the general public. They also provide classes on genealogy and one-on-one assistance to inexperienced family historians. Here you will find a **Complete Listing of Delaware Family History Centers**.

Complete Listing of Delaware Family History Centers:
https://familysearch.org/locations/centerlocator

Additional Delaware Genealogical Resources

Delaware Mailing Lists

Mailing lists are internet based facilities that use email to distribute a single message to all who subscribe to it. When information on a particular surname, new records, or any other important genealogy information related to the mailing list topic becomes available, the subscribers are alerted to it. Joining a mailing list is an excellent way to stay up to date on Delaware genealogy research topics. Rootsweb have an extensive listing of **Delaware Mailing Lists** on a variety of topics.

Delaware Mailing Lists:
http://lists.rootsweb.ancestry.com/index/usa/DE/misc.html

Delaware Message Boards

A message board is another internet based facility where people can post questions about a specific genealogy topic and have it answered by other genealogists. If you have questions about a surname, record type, or research topic, you can post your question and other researchers and genealogists will help you with the answer. Be sure to check back regularly, as the answers are not emailed to you. The Delaware Message Boards at **Rootsweb** are completely free to use.

Rootsweb:
http://boards.rootsweb.com/localities.northam.usa.states/mb.ashx

Delaware Newspapers and Periodicals

Many genealogy periodicals and historical newspapers contain reprinted copies of family genealogies, transcripts of family Bible records, information about local records and archives, census indexes, church records, queries, land records, obituaries, court records, cemetery records, and wills. The following sites have historical Delaware newspapers and periodicals that you can search online or on-site.

The Historical Society of Delaware Library – periodicals and journals

The Historical Society of Delaware Library: http://www.hsd.org/

University of Delaware Library – hundreds of historical and current newspapers dating from the 19th century

University of Delaware Library; http://www2.lib.udel.edu/delnews/list.htm

NewspaperArchive.com – largest online database of historical newspapers in the world.

NewspaperArchive.com: http://newspaperarchive.com/

Historical Delaware Maps and Gazetteers

Maps are an integral part of genealogical research. They help us to locate landmarks, towns, cities, parishes, states, provinces, waterways and roads and streets. They also help us to determine when and where boundary changes might have taken place, and give us a visualization of the area we're researching in. For locating place names, a gazetteer is the best possible resource for any genealogist. Gazetteers are also sometimes called "place name dictionaries", and can help you to locate the area in which you need to conduct research. Below are links to the maps and gazetteers for research in Delaware.

Peabody GNIS Service – Delaware:
http://peabody.research.yale.edu/cgi-bin/Query.GNIS?ST=Delaware&SU=1

Color Landform Atlas – Delaware:
http://fermi.jhuapl.edu/states/de_0.html

1985 U.S. Atlas: http://www.livgenmi.com/1895/DE/

Delaware Hometown Locator:
http://delaware.hometownlocator.com/

Delaware City Directories
.

City directories are similar to telephone directories in that they list the residents of a particular area. The difference though is what is important to genealogists, and that is they pre-date telephone directories. You can find an ancestor's information such as their street address, place of employment, occupation, or the name of their spouse. A one-stop-shop for finding city directories in Delaware is the **Delaware Online Historical Directories** which contains a listing of every available city and historical directory related to Delaware.

Delaware Online Historical Directories:
https://sites.google.com/site/onlinedirectorysite/Home/usa/de

University of Delaware Library – Variety of City directories for Delaware and several surrounding states

> 181 South College Avenue
> Newark, DE 19717-5267 USA
> Phone: (302) 831-2965

University of Delaware Library:
http://guides.lib.udel.edu/c.php?g=85348&p=548268

Delaware Public Archives- Wilmington City Directories 1814-1974

Delaware Public Archives:
http://archives.delaware.gov/collections/guide/9000S/9215-1.shtml

Delaware Genealogical Records

<u>Birth, Death, Marriage and Divorce Records</u> – Birth, death, and marriage records are the most basic, yet most important records attached to your ancestor. They are generally referred to as vital records as they record vital life events. The reason for their importance is that they not only place your ancestor in a specific place at a definite time, but potentially connect the individual to other relatives. Below is a list of repositories and websites where you can find Delaware vital records

Delaware Office of Vital Statistics - birth, death, marriage, same-gender marriage, adoptee, and civil union certificates

Delaware Office of Vital Statistics:
http://www.dhss.delaware.gov/dph/ss/vitalstats.html

Delaware Public Archives - birth, death, marriage, divorce, and veterans certificates older than 72 years

Delaware Public Archives:
http://www.delaware.gov/topics/certificates

Delaware State Birth Records, 1861-1922

Delaware State Birth Records, 1861-1922:
https://familysearch.org/search/collection/1534607

Delaware Marriages, 1713-1919

Delaware Marriages, 1713-1919:
https://familysearch.org/search/collection/1674782

Delaware Deaths and Burials, 1815-1955

Delaware Deaths and Burials, 1815-1955:
https://familysearch.org/search/collection/1674781

Census Reports

Census records are among the most important genealogical documents for placing your ancestor in a particular place at a specific time. Like BDM records, they can also lead you to other ancestors, particularly those who were living under the authority of the head of household.

Delaware census records exist from 1790-1910 and many images and indexes can be viewed online. Following are the best places to find Delaware census records.

Delaware Public Archives – census records from 1790

Delaware Public Archives:
http://archives.delaware.gov/collections/census.shtml

U.S National Archives – Federal census records on microfilm available from 1790 to 1940.

U.S National Archives: http://www.archives.gov/research/census/

AccessGenealogy – Delaware Census records from 1880-1930

AccessGenealogy:
http://www.accessgenealogy.com/census/delaware-1790-1930-census-records.htm

Delaware Church Records

Church and synagogue records are a valuable resource, especially for baptisms, marriages, and burials that took place before 1900. You will need to at least have an idea of your ancestor's religious denomination, and in most cases you will have to visit a brick and mortar establishment to view them.

Most church records are kept by the individual church, although in some denominations, records are placed in a regional archive or maintained at the diocesan level. Local Historical Societies are sometimes the repository for the state's older church records. Below are links archives that maintain church records, as well as a few databases that can be viewed online.

The **Family History Library** contains many church records from a variety of denominations on microfilm.

Family History Library:
http://familysearch.org/learn/wiki/en/Family_History_Library

The **University of Delaware Library** has a massive collection of multi-denominational church records including baptisms, births, deaths, burials, and marriages

University of Delaware Library:
http://guides.lib.udel.edu/content.php?pid=164045&sid=1840549

The **Delaware Historical Society Church and Cemetery Folder Collection** - contains information from churches throughout the entire state of Delaware that includes member rolls, baptisms, marriages, burial records, pew holders, and much more

Delaware Historical Society Church and Cemetery Folder Collection:
http://www.hsd.org/Library/Church_CemeteryFolder/DeHisSociety_Church_Cemetery_Folder.htm

Central Repositories for Denominational Records

Most of the records of individual denominations are kept in central repositories. Below is a list of the major congregational archives in Delaware, links to their websites, physical addresses, and contact information.

Methodist

United Methodist Archives Center
Drew University
36 Madison Ave.
Madison, NJ 07940-4007
Tel: (973) 408-3125
Fax: (973) 408-3770

United Methodist Archives Center:
http://www.gcah.org/site/pp.aspx?c=ghKJI0PHIoE&b=3590193

Presbyterian

The Presbyterian Historical Society
425 Lombard Street
Philadelphia, PA 19147-1516
Tel: (215) 627-1852
Fax: (215) 627-0509

The Presbyterian Historical Society: http://www.history.pcusa.org/

Roman Catholic

Diocese of Wilmington Archives
P.O. Box 2030
Greenville, DE 19899
Tel: (302) 655-0597

Diocese of Wilmington Archives:
http://www.cdow.org/archives.html

Society of Friends (Quaker)

Friends Historical Library
Swarthmore College
500 College Avenue
Swarthmore, PA 19081-1399
Telephone: (610) 328-8496
Fax: (610) 690-5728
E-mail: friends@swarthmore.edu

Friends Historical Library:
http://www.swarthmore.edu/academics/friends-historical-library.xml

Delaware Military Records

More than 40 million Americans have participated in some time of war service since America was colonized. The chance of finding your ancestor amongst those records is exceptionally high. Military records can even reveal individuals who never actually served, such as those who registered for the two World Wars but were never called to duty.

Below are a number of links to websites and archives that contain Delaware military records.

University of Delaware Library – regimental histories from King George's War, 1744-1748; French and Indian War, 1755-1763; Revolutionary War, 1775-1783, and War of 1812, plus officers lists and military histories

University of Delaware Library:
http://guides.lib.udel.edu/content.php?pid=164045&sid=2237926

Delaware Public Archives – huge collection of Revolutionary War records that include pensions lists, pension receipt books, veterans accounts, correspondences, loyalists records, plus War of 1812 records, militia records for 1765 to 1841, Mexican Border dispute, Civil War files, Spanish-American War, National Guard Card File, World War I, and World War II records.

Delaware Public Archives:
http://archives.delaware.gov/collections/revolutionary%20war%20re
cord/revguiderev.shtml

U.S. National Archives – WWI Draft registration cards, casualties lists, WWI and WWII service records, Korean War records, Vietnam War records, Civil War and Spanish-American War records, and casualties lists.

U.S. National Archives:
http://www.archives.gov/research/military/veterans/online.html

United States Index to Indian Wars Pension Files, 1892-1926 – military pension records of soldiers who fought in the Indian Wars between 1817 and 1898

United States Index to Indian Wars Pension Files, 1892-1926: https://familysearch.org/search/collection/1979427

United States Mexican War Pension Index, 1887-1926 - index to Mexican War pension files for service between 1846 and 1848

United States Mexican War Pension Index, 1887-1926: https://familysearch.org/search/collection/1979390

Civil War Soldiers Service Records - Service records for both Union and Confederate soldiers indexed by soldier's name, rank, and unit.

Civil War Soldier Service Records: http://go.fold3.com/civilwar_records/

Delaware Cemetery Records

As convenient as it is to search cemetery records online, keep in mind that there are a few disadvantages over visiting a cemetery in person. They are:

- Tombstone information is not always accurately transcribed
- The arrangement of the graves in a cemetery can be crucial as family members are often buried next to each other or in the same grave. This arrangement is not always preserved in the alphabetical indexes that are found online.

With that information in mind, the following websites have databases that can be searched online for Delaware Cemetery records.

Delaware Tombstone Transcription Project - death and burial records

Delaware Tombstone Transcription Project:
http://usgwtombstones.org/delaware/delaware.html

African American Cemeteries Online – African American, slave, and Native American cemetery records

African American Cemeteries Online:
http://africanamericancemeteries.com/ar/

Access Genealogy – huge database of delaware cemetery record transcriptions

Access Genealogy:
http://www.accessgenealogy.com/cemetery/delaware.htm

Find a Grave – over 100 million grave records can be searched on this site. Search can be conducted by name, location, or cemetery name.

Find a Grave: http://www.findagrave.com/

Interment.net - A free online database containing approximately 4 million cemetery records from around the world.

Interment.net: http://www.interment.net/

Billion Graves – as the name implies, you can search a billion records including headstone photos, transcriptions, cemetery records, and grave locations.

Billion Graves:
http://billiongraves.com/pages/search/index.php#cemetery

Delaware Obituaries

Obituaries can reveal a wealth about our ancestor and other relatives. You can search our **Delaware Newspaper Obituaries Listings** from hundreds of Delaware newspapers online for free.

Delaware Newspaper Obituaries Listings:
http://obituarieshelp.org/delaware_newspaper_obituaries.html

Delaware Wills and Probate Records

The documents found in a probate packet may include a complete inventory of a person's estate, newspaper entries, witness testimony, a copy of a will, list of debtors and creditors, names of executors or trustees, names of heirs. They can not only tell you about the ancestor you're currently researching, but lead to other ancestors. Most of these records must be accessed at a county court or clerk's office, but some can be found online as well. You can obtain copies of the original probate records by writing to the county clerk.

Delaware Public Archives – probate records for the entire state dating from 1680 to 1925. Collection includes records from the Swedish colonial period, the Dutch settlement, the Duke of York, and the Penn proprietorship.

Delaware Public Archives:
http://archives.delaware.gov/collections/probate.shtml

University of Delaware Library – indexes to Sussex County, Delaware Probate Records, 1680-1800, Kent County, Delaware Probate Records, 1680-1800, Calendar of Delaware Wills, New Castle County, 1682-1800, New Castle County, Delaware Wills, 1682-1800

University of Delaware Library:
http://guides.lib.udel.edu/content.php?pid=164045&sid=3339526

Delaware Immigration and Naturalization Records

The naturalization process generated many types of records, including petitions, declarations of intention, and oaths of allegiance. These records can provide family historians with information such as a person's birth date and place of birth, immigration year, marital status, spouse information, occupation, witnesses' names and addresses, and more.

Naturalization Records Database – Searchable online index of naturalization records for Newcastle, Kent, and Sussex counties searchable by place or name.

Naturalization Records Database:
http://archives.delaware.gov/collections/natrlzndb/nat-index.shtml

Delaware, County Naturalization Records, 1796-1958 - records and digitized indexes from county courthouses

Delaware, County Naturalization Records, 1796-1958:
https://familysearch.org/search/collection/2057672

US National Archives – Naturalization records 1845-1910, and Ships Passenger Lists for 1845-1910 Wilmington arrivals

US National Archives:
http://www.archives.gov/research/immigration/passenger-arrival.html

Delaware Native American Records

Access Genealogy – Native American census records, tribal histories, and much more

Access Genealogy: http://www.accessgenealogy.com/native/

Midwest Genealogy Center – a wide variety of records from the vast majority of Native American tribes in the United States on microfilm

Midwest Genealogy Center
3440 S. Lee's Summit Road
Independence, Missouri

Midwest Genealogy Center:
http://www.mymcpl.org/_uploaded_resources/MGC-micronatamer.pdf

The **National Archives** - information about American Indians who maintained their ties to Federally-recognized Tribes (1830-1970).

National Archives: http://www.archives.gov/research/native-americans/

Bureau of Indian Affairs

Bureau of Indian Affairs: http://www.bia.gov/

Missing Matriarchs – Resources for Researching Female Delaware Ancestors

Looking for female ancestors requires an adjustment of how we view traditional records sources. A woman's identity was often under that of her husband, and often individual records for them can be difficult to locate. The following resources are effective in locating female ancestors in Delaware where traditional records may not reveal them.

Marriage and Divorce Records

Marriages were first recorded by the county beginning in 1680. It wasn't until 1847 that state-wide registration began however, and that was not completely enforced until 1913. Any records before 1930 are held at the Hall of Records in Dover. Those records issued after 1930 are at the Office of Vital Statistics, also in Dover. The neighbouring states of Maryland and Pennsylvania also hold some Delaware marriage records.

Divorces that took place before 1897 were handled by the Delaware Legislative Council, though they continued to grant divorces until 1906. After 1900 jurisdiction was given to the Superior Court and those records are held by individual counties.

The following indexes can be found at the Hall of Records in Dover on microfilm:

1. Marriage Card index, 1680-1850 (film 0006416 ff.)
2. Marriage Records, 1865-1954 (film 2025062 ff.)
3. Clerk of the Peace Marriage bonds, 1865-1861 and licenses, 1889-1894 (film 0006412 ff.)

The **Delaware Historical Society** holds the following records:

1. County marriage records and licenses, 1680-1850
2. Brandywine Hundred marriages, 1836-1909
3. Wilmington marriage registers, 1856-1864
4. Miscellaneous Delaware marriage licenses, 1902-present

5. Marriage license applications for the Middletown area, 1926-1935

Delaware Historical Society link to: http://www.hsd.org/gengd.htm

<u>Bibliographies</u>

- *Delaware Genealogical Research Guide,* Thomas Doherty (Delaware Genealogical Society, 1997)
- *Loosening the bonds: Mid-Atlantic Farm Women, 1758-1850* Joan M. Jensen (Yale University Press, 1986)
- *Genealogical Abstracts from the Biographical and Genealogical History of the State of Delaware,* Bill and Martha Reamy (Family Line Publications, 1998)
- *Women in the City of Brotherly Love and Beyond: Tours and Detours in Delaware Valley Women's History,* Gayle B. Samuels (The Author, 1994)
- *Guide to Women's History Resources in the Delaware Valley,* Trina Vaux (University of Pennsylvania Press, 1984)

Selected Resources for Delaware Women's History

Women's Research Center
University of Delaware
Political Science Department
Newark, DE 19716

Winterthur Museum and library
Route 52, Kenneth Pike
Winterthur, DE 19735

Common Delaware Surnames

The following surnames are among the most common in Delaware. The list is by no means exhaustive. If your surname doesn't appear in the list it doesn't mean that you have no Delaware connections, only that your surname may be less common. These are names that are also being currently researched in Delaware, so if you do find your surname here, there is a chance that some research has already been performed on your ancestor.

Adams, Anderson, Andreozzi, Andrews, Aye, Bailey, Baldwin, Balh, Balles, Banning, Baxley, Beardsley, Behle, Berger, Beyer, Blain, Blakeslee, Bloomer, Blose, Boas, Borque, Bower, Bowler, Boyce, Bradish, Brenneman, Briggs, Brown, Burton, Bush, Caddis, Caldwell, Calhoun, Carey, Carruthers, Cartier, Casey, Cathers, Clements, Collins, Cooper, Cordrey, Coulbourn,Crothers, Crouch, Culver, Curtis, Daisey, Daly, Davis, Dernehl, Derrickson, Desy, DeVaughn, Dickinson, Diehl, Dixon, Donovan, Doyon, Duhme, Earnest, Elliott, Ellis, Elzey, Emmert, English, Evans, Exley, Fancher, Fischer, Fisher, Fleck, Flemer, Fluamer, Flummer, Foos,Foskey, Frame, Furlong, Geis, Glass, Golt, Gordy, Green, Greg, Greim, Groninger, Gropp, Haag, Hall, Hammond, Harwin, Hasting, Hastings, Hawk, Hearn, Hearne, Hellens, Herzog, Hickman, Hill, Hoffmann, Hogg, Hollingsworth, Horn, House, Houston, Hudson, Hughes,Hummell, Iddings, Inloes, Japes, Johnson, Jones, Julien, Kauffman, Keen, Kennerly, Kenney, Kerney, Kearney, Kerr, Kimberly, King, Kinneken, Kinsey, Klang, Knightly, Knipe, Knowles, Lantz, Larimore, Lariviere, Lasbury, LeCates, Lenney, Lennon, Leslie, Lewis, Lindell, Lindsay, Lishman, Lister, Lyons, Maasch, Mackey, Macklin, Malloy, Matthews, May, McCarthy, McGarrity, Mears, Melson, Mettee, Metzger, Mills, Minnich, Montigny, Montour, Morgan, Morris, Mueller, Murgatroyd, Murray, Myers, Nash, Neale, Neels, Newlin, Oman, Orrell, Page, Painter, Paynter, Parks, Passwaters, Payne, Pehrsson, Penton, Peterson, Philley, Phillips, Pierce, Pigott, Pontius, Pontious, Posten, Pratt, Pugh, Purchase, Purnell, Pusey,

Quillia, Reddick, Reed, Regli, Reynolds, Richardson, Rickards, Roche, Rodgers, Rogers, Rumbaugh, Schneider, Schulte, Shepley, Shockley, Short, Sinnott, Sischell, Slattery, Snell, Spence, Spicer, Spurgeon, Starr, Sweeney, Tatro, Tierlinck, Tilden, Tingle, Toohey, Travilla, Truby, Truitt, Tubbs, Tucke,r Tunnell, Tyndall, Underwood, Underwood, Van Thorre, Vaughn, Voshell, Warren, Waud, Weaver, Williams, Welsh, West, Whitebread, Wiles, Willey, Wilson, Wise, Wolf, Wolfrey, Woolfrey, Wood, Woodman, Workman, Wright, Wyatt, Yale, Yelle, Zeth

About the Author

Gary L. Morris worked from 2009 to 2014 as a professional researcher for a major player in the genealogy field. After tracing his family lineage back to 1683, he found that genealogy could be an expensive undertaking. As such, has decided to publish these helpful guides to share the valuable free information he has discovered during his career to help others trace their family lineages as inexpensively as possible. An avid genealogist himself, he hopes you will find this guide factual, thorough, helpful, and most of all, effective in helping you to find your family members.